Twelve Kentucky Poets

Cathy Gilbert, Ken Hageman, Jessica Patterson,
Alex Lanter, Hannah Lewis, Donna Lee Campbell,
Sarizel LeFevers Robbins, Charlotte Irene Ingram,
Hannah Rhea Marsh, Shad Smith,
and Ron Whitehead

Wasteland Press
Louisville, KY USA
www.wastelandpress.com

the literary renaissance
Louisville, KY USA
www.tappingmyownphone.com
www.literaryocean.blogspot.com

a Published In Heaven Book
for the literary renaissance

Twelve Kentucky Poets
By Cathy Gilbert, Ken Hageman, Jessica Patterson,
Alex Lanter, Hannah Lewis, Donna Lee Campbell,
Sarizel LeFevers Robbins, Charlotte Irene Ingram,
Hannah Rhea Marsh, Shad Smith,
and Ron Whitehead

First Printing-March, 2003
Back cover photos by Ken Hageman
Book design by Wasteland Press

ISBN: 0-9729186-7-1

Printed In The U.S.A.

Twelve Kentucky Poets

Table Of Contents

Cathy Gilbert

Point in Time

I own this river,
diamonds dancing on her light belong to me.
The sun sets because I am here to see.
A soft breeze whispers, my memory.
This place the Lord hath made,
the best things in life are free.

Bird's Eye View

It is sitting in the middle of 227.
What must things look like from there?
Monster squashing machines coming at you from both directions.
It must be scared to death.

I would be.

Good Grief.
Pull over. Pop the trunk. Put on gloves. Stop traffic. Pick it up.
Now what.

Doesn't appear to be injured.
Just can't fly.
I can, but only in my dreams.

Let's sit you down in this grassy spot.
I've heard most of the time you are just stunned from the impact.
After you get your wits you will be okay.
I'm like that too.

We are getting more alike all the time.

Look! Look! Look! Go! Go! Go!

You only needed a few minutes to steady your balance.
We could all use a hand up when we are down.

Goodbye feathered friend.

I will fly with you in my dreams.

I wonder about the Bible verse where God watches over the sparrow.
He surely is today.

War

Stock market soars
Blood pours
The war machine roars
Craving death and dollars

Better Late Than Never

Blow out the candles. Make a wish.
I wish for my period to come.

Thirty-four years ago I did not want it to come.
I did not want breasts. I did not want hair.
I certainly did not want my period.

After a few months I hated it still.
I told my mother, "If I am in an accident be sure they remove my
ovaries. Even if I break my leg, remove my ovaries."

For thirty-four years the period comes, the period goes
except for the summer of '73.

Happy 47th Birthday to me.
I wish my period would come.
I am worried about perimenopause.
It's early but women my age have already seen signs.
Like missing a period.
Mine is late.

Now I love my period.

Hot flashes?
Please don't get me started.

Angela's Ashes

In Memory of Angela Dawson (1966-2002)

"Mass destruction?
Tell the president to come to this drug-infested hellhole if he wants to
see weapons of mass destruction.

Angela was a good neighbor.
Good kids. Carnell Jr., Juan, the twins Kevin and Keith and LaWanda.
Even her man Carnell Sr. was okay by me.
Now they're all dead. Murdered. Burned up. That's mass destruction.
That's terrorism. I'm poor white trash. What do I know.

Angela called the law on the goddamn dealers.
She testified down to the courthouse.
She thought she'd stand up. Now she's dead. Her husband and her five
kids. Dead. Murdered. Burned up.

Said in the paper Baltimore's the worst city in the country.
Drugs everygoddamnwhere.
I never lived nowhere but here. What do I know.

That sonofabitch Darrell Brooks kicked in the front door and torched
Angela's home.
All them upstairs sleeping. After he done firebombed her three weeks
ago.

What's this shit about no child left behind? All children left to die here.
Terrorism. Shit. Don't tell me about terrorism.
Out my window is under siege.

Tell the president
 he's invited to my house for toast and tea. Sprinkled with Angela's
ashes."

Fear of flies

I was afraid of flies when I was three.
I became a siren.
The fly would be gone
but once I turned on
it was hell to turn me off.

My mom was at her wit's end.
The screaming had to stop.
Sitting by my tricycle
she prepared me for its landing.

With conviction she said, "I want you to look at this fly.
I am right here beside you."
Face to face with the hideous monster
I whispered, "He's got pink pedal pushers on."

Desire

Lightning bore my sexuality
Three powerhouse forces of nature
I am Eve

Kathryn's Fall II

I remember how intensely she guards her privacy.
How will she react to my words about her life?
I hold my breath for two minutes watching her read.
There is a frown, then a hint of a smile
and a tear.

"People say I am hard headed," she says.
"But you didn't tell them about the cats."
I am breathing again.
Tommy and Johnny stayed on Kathryn's belly

as she lay in the field with a broken hip.

They kept her company watching the Big Dipper
and falling stars all that cold, wet night.
The strong-willed, redheaded Irish woman loves her cats.
On that night, as many before and since, they saved her life.
I am thankful Kathryn helped me remember the rest of the story.

Don't You Get It

Until then it was a routine stop
at Cowboys
to fill up and get coffee.

A young woman was talking on the pay phone.
I did not mean to be eavesdropping
but she was pretty loud.

From her angry expression
 it was obvious
she was arguing with her insignificant other.

"DON'T YOU GET IT? I DON'T WANT YOU ANYMORE."

 It was the flashback that shocked me.

 I don't know who that fella was
 or where he was
 but for that moment
 I wish I could have beamed myself through the line
 to hold on to him.

Maybe he was a good guy or maybe not.
I would have held on to him.
I know he was knocked down.

Those words hurt like hell
and this time I wasn't in the line of fire.

I thought about it for a long time.
I don't ever want to hear those words screamed at me again.

The Good Lord Works in Mysterious Ways

In Memory of Louise Boyd

Louise volunteered in the Army of the Lord.
She may not have known that she served.

On Sunday mornings not so many years ago
it was Louise who inspired me to put on my face
and maybe a hat
to take my place in the second row.

Louise was ruthless with her secret weapon
delivered in an unassuming sack labeled "Cathy."
Not every Sunday but on very good Sundays
Louise brought me homemade cookies.

A better baker God never made.
On each attack she deployed a simply irresistible recipe.

Many a preacher and good parishioner has tried
to lure me through the front door.
But Louise, wise woman that she was,
knew the power of chocolate and love.

We pray for the day when all battles fought in the name of the Lord
can be won by such a delicious war strategy.

Ken Hageman

Insight
(I am not the Poem)

I am not the poem,
>I'm not the sonnet of sadness
>The song of empty shadows
>The silhouette of faded sunsets

I am a simple man of self conjecture

I am not the poem
>I'm not Richard The Lionhearted
>Napoleon Columbus
>Alexander The Great

I am a simple man of inner exploration

I am not the poem
>I'm not the man they thought I was
>They think I am
>They think I will be

I'm a simple man unfounded in their beliefs

I am not the poem
>I'm not the poet
>The thinker
>The wise man
>The believer

I am a simple man who sees what he sees

I am not the poem
>I'm not you, but like you
>Him
>Her
>We...

I am not the poem
>The poem is me

Whispers of rose petals

(Tic-Tac-Toe)

If she says she loves me,
        I say she loves me not!
If she says she loves me,
        I say she loves me not!
Both holding stem hand in hand,
        Only one petal stands
Who gets the last whisper?...
        (please!! let it be her!!)
            (I was only playing hard to get)
Then... the wind blows
        The game is over...
She smiles softly
        And quietly walks away
(stick of thorns in hand I am left bleeding from a game I never seem to win)

Thanks for Nothing

And silence befell the young man
Whence given a chance
To address the
World
Merely a whisper let out,
Yet incessant screams within
He smiled and thanked
the microphone politely
Walking away he chanted...
"Let e'm know,
or let it go."
"Let e'm know,
or let it go!!"

Over four billion served
(Service with a smile)

My dad can beat up your dad!
My leader says your leader is "unfit" to lead

Put down your weapons and walk away!
Only WE, the responsible...
                    Are allowed to toy with
Mass Destruction

Here have some food you don't like,
Some freedom you didn't ask for,
2,000 years of tradition
You don't know what you're miss'n,
Big macks are better than "*misguided*" virtues
Any ol' day.
So "have a coke and a smile"
or I'll tell my dad.

Reincarnation

What has brought me to the brink of self-recreation
Like dead skin the dry and flaky dreams of yesterday
 must be brushed away.
The lotion of reality must be applied generously
Lightly rubbed in a circular motion
To soothe and regenerate a new destiny
The calloused scars of personal past
Will never completely fade
But with time they will blend.
Let this new day of dreams anticipation
Full of life and saturation
 Bring me like a newborn
Fresh from the womb
Is your water breaking?

THE AWAKENING

Awaken to the window,
of your self-created shelter.
This window is the only opening,
In your self-erected walls of insecurities,
and self-consciousness,
Through which
you watch your real life pass you by.
For within
All you have is what you have,
As you look out
You see all that you are afraid to get.
Breathe one last breath
of the stale air of cubical security
and thrust open your window.
Now step through, unto a new awakening;
For a real Life has no walls.

My Children
(How Shall I Hold Them)

My Children will be mine, even if they are someone else's.
My children shall be held.
My children can be male or female it makes no difference.
They will be equal in my eyes, regardless,
My children will be loved, at all times, and they will know it, at all
costs.
My children will not be perfect, and they will understand.
My children will be intelligent, to the utmost of their abilities.
My children will have common sense.
My children will be respectful and polite.
My children will be disciplined, by me, and by themselves.
My children will do chores and have responsibilities
My children will have their phases of laziness.
My children will be spoiled, spoiled more with love than with material
things,
But none the less they will be spoiled.

My children will respect nature, and have great experiences out of doors.

My children shall be held.

My children won't always like me, but they will always love me.

My children will love flowers, I will give flowers to them,

My children will give flowers to others,

Flowers and butterflies will be a game that we play,

Butterflies by day, fireflies by night.

My children will climb trees, I shall climb trees with them.

My children will have a tire swing just as I did,

I will watch them out the back window playing in their swing.

My children shall be my teacher, I shall do my best to teach them.

My children shall never meet their grandmother, yet they shall know her still,

They shall feel her love,

They shall hear her laughter,

My children will be held.

My children will have lots of friends, I hope that I am one of them.

My children will be adventuress, in their own way.

My children will have a dog.

My children will read books, I shall read books to them.

My children will build snowmen at least once, and see the ocean as well.

My children will have hobbies, I shall have hobbies with them.

My children won't have everything, but they will have everything they need.

My children will be active in school, and I shall be there to see.

My children will fight with each other, but they will be each other's best friends.

My children will be sheltered, my children shall be exposed.

My children shall have no prejudice through no fault of my own.

My children will cry, I shall cry for my children.

My children will know that drugs aren't evil,

But they can be destructive, and they **will** rob you of your youth.

My children will know that sex and love are two different things

But should they ever find that they have both, marry.

As my children grow older, they will still be my children,

I will still be their friend.

My children will know that knowledge is one of the few true possessions,

It cannot be taken away by conventional means.

My children shall be independent,

She will be strong,
He will be sensitive,
Both shall be aware.
My children shall be president if they choose,
My children will be heroes if they believe.
My children shall have a sense of direction sooner than I.
My children will be pressured to always do their best,
And held even closer when their best still wasn't good enough.
My children will know that making a difference in the world is optional,
Being happy is mandatory,
And that success is measured by the latter.
My children will make me proud, just being my children.
My children will love their mother as I,
My children will know their father if it is not me.
My children will read this book and know that I tried my best, for my children
My children shall cry at my funeral.
My children, how shall I hold them?
As close as I can,
As long as they will allow,

And still closer after that!

Hello ?!!

Empty sickness
The prelude to epiphany
Moments before
The breakdown
The "Bowdown"
In intimate
And/or
Angry
Conversation with
Your God!

"Seek and ye shall find"
And his compassion healed all-the-world,
one anguished soul at a time.

?
(Empty Echoes)

Dad,

    Dad,

        Dad!!

            Dad?...

                Da-ad??

                    Daaad?!!....

                        Da-a-ad??

                            Dad?...

                                Dad.

                                      Dad.

                                          D.

                                              ?

Who owns this kid
Game boy

Who holds the tongue of the little blue boy
Our children are not born monsters
They are born babies
In a monstrosity we call civilization,
Minus the civil
add exaggeration of the dramatization
12 hours a day on a video game
killing everything that moves

"hit points" not "grade points"
set the ambiance of their mood.
Guns don't kill people-children do
"accidentally" of course
after all what do you think they are?...
Monsters???
if that's the case just leave them at the department store
or beat them senseless when you get back to the car
who needs love to occupy their time
when there are hundreds of cartridges for that
game

TEARS IN THE WIND

Awaken to Mother Earth, take heed of her despair,
We hear her silent screams, yet no one seems to care.
We see her starving masses, we watch her dying breeds,
Ravaged and plundered by the concept of greed.
With the closing of the eye, or the turning of the head,
Another forest gone, another species dead.
Now the clouds bring not rain, but tears unto the Earth,
Saddened by her destruction, she weeps about her birth.
For she was once young and strong, breathing winds so fresh and free
With flowers in every field, fruit on every tree.
Her rivers and her oceans were once clear as clear could be,
When you gaze upon them now you'll see pollution and debris.
The birds no longer rule the sky nor the fishes rule the sea,
Taken away was their majestic throne, for the convenience of you and me.
To make life a little easier, what a sacrifice we've made,
For the rainbows now are just one color; A gray and dismal shade.
What will we tell our grandchildren, when they sit upon our knee,
Asking with their puzzled eyes, why flower cease to be.
Still her calls will go unanswered, thought they ring through sea and land,
The excuses all the same, I'm too busy to lend a hand.
And as the teardrops continue falling, from the clouds within her eyes,
I have to stop and wonder, will her life soon pass us by?
Will there be a breath; one last breath; before she crumbles into space,

I think of all her wasted beauty, as the tears roll down my face,
Yet the tears will go unnoticed as they collect upon my chin,
for my tear, mixed with her tears,
will be scattered
in the
wind.

Jessica Patterson

GRANDMOTHER

One day I stopped upon a hill to pray
'Bout why my grandmother couldn't play
I moped and moaned up there all day
And then returned at night to stay
Dear Lord, please help her, I meant to say
Because my grandmother cannot stay
Please keep her safe by night and day
I beg and plead and still I pray
Oh why-oh why-must she pay
For living and loving from day to day
She's been the bringer of joy and peace
The giver and keeper of joy and feasts
And yet she lies in pain unceased
And yet we'll love her-for life is leased.

HOUSING AND HOMES

Frame it up straight and cover with wood;
Tack on a roof-to make it good.
Deck all the walls with paintings of glory;
Or just kick back and watch a movie.
Move in the cozies and fill it with love-
That's not a house! It's what a home's made of.

LIGHT

Soft; soothing; pale; glimmering;
Multi-shadowed, sweetly shimmering;
Warm, sizzling, simmering.
Harsh; loud;popping;buzzing;
Silent cloud; blissful fuzzing;
Is the basement light bulbing-
With a bright fire sparkling.

GREEN

Green with envy
Green with hate
Green with jealousy-the bait!
Green in Spring
Green on grass
Green on trees-through the glass.
Green in summer
Green on breeze
Green of weeds-makes me sneeze~
Green of Pine
Green of Oak
Green of Nature-is no joke!
Green on halter
Green on rope
Green on saddle pad-please note-
Green on hocks
Green on knees
Green on buttocks-if you please...
Green am I-that's my color
Green I love like no other!

DEATH-THE GREAT TRAGEDY

I got up in the morning to a bright sunny day,
And looked out the window to see the horses play-
I sat on the porch with my first cup of joe
And thought well isn't it nice to watch the grass grow!
I walked to the barn to feed the herd-
And stepped in a big ol' smelly turd.
I looked to the field to see what I could;
And wouldn't you know- a big stick of wood.
I walked out to it, for I couldn't see-
Some trash from the neighbors-that could be.
That's not what it is- nestled in a grassy bed-
Oh, NO! Not TRUE! That foal is dead.

THAT'S MY DAY

As I sit and contemplate of what this day to make-
I feel the rhythms of the place within my bones I shake.

I feel the peace of furnace blowing; yet still knowing-
Lying there-the cat's displeasure for his ears are feathered.

At work the critters holler- for more food and water-
Music blares; the phone is ringing and the bird is singing.

In the barn horses nicker-then the lihgt bulbs flicker-
Soft hay rustling-with soft noses nuzzling.

Home again-that's my day-now it's time for me to play!

BIRTHDAY PRESENT

When I came home,
Beside the road I stopped to play.
Whistling through teeth-I walked.
When home-I stopped;
Stopped beside the road to ponder-
Why my heart thunders!
That's not my heart I thought-
That's the sound-of hooves on high!
The whistle in my ears I hear...
Is the trumpet of a mare!
Is it mine-I stopped to wonder?
Why sure-it's my birthday!

PRAYER

Bless me, my Father, my God, my radical redeemer.
Support me, my Savior, for this world is meaner.
Guide me, my Father, for I'm a great dreamer.

Cherish me, my Savior, for all time meanders.

Support all, my Savior, for this world we smash.
Guide all, my Father, so we won't stray from Your path.
Cherish all, my Savior, for we'll be the last.

Support us, my Savior, for we're coming home.
Guide us, my Father, till we see Your great throne.
Cherish us, my Savior, for we are your own.
Bless us all, my Father, my God, my radical redeemer.

And Jesus said:

"Ask, and it shall be given you; seek, and ye shall find;
knock, and it shall be opened unto you: For every one
that asketh receiveth; and he that seeketh findeth; and
to him that knocketh it shall be opened."
Matthew 7:7-8 KJV

BUNKS

I always yearned
dreamed

of brother's bunk
bed

of deep varnished
wood

clothed in soft
blankets

I could not
sleep

in brother's bunk
bed

for my mother's
fear

of my falling

I REMEMBER

I remember pain and sedition; unending strife and oppression;
Anxious days to look forward to with nervous trepidation;
Fear and doubt haunted my every childish decision;
Despair wracked and tortured me with every familial inquisition.

I remember warm golden days; bees in the summer;
An escape to a glorious fantasy from my father-or mother.
Lying in the grass, my young heart bursting asunder;
Dreaming of peaceful completion with a yet unknown lover.

I remember love and confusion; dust and delusion;
Grassy meadows of peaceful profusion.
Thundering emotion with mean locomotion-
Those days were mine-yet showed my devotion.

REFLECTIONS ON IRAQ

God bless the war
that brings down the demon
of the state of the downtrodden.

Let the war be crushed
that unholy engine
that would destroy the people.

Going to war with Iraq-
we win-we lose-
and just why should we care?

LIFE

Life is nothing if not
a breath away
from total oblivion.

Alex Lanter

Tragic Mirth

Tragic mirth
Chafing my heart my soul
Vexed again
Unfrequented rooms echo hollow ambition

Nettle stings black anxiety
Piercing with sharp point
Old wounds made new
Revisited with pale regret

In sunken hollow vacant chest
Cry pangs of love
Mournful dread melancholy congeal my blood
Provoking my soul to fret on things once in reach

Distant beckoning tasks me
Past remembered future unseen
Passion weighs in heavy decline
In darkness despondency blooms

Reconnoiter existence in search of hope
To fill the frightful void
To ignite other's concupiscence in my wake
Escaping trial's disdain.

Turns out of plumb

My mind turns an elegant gasp
At beauty once beheld
Thoughts of what might have been
Stampede through my brain
Absent joys drill holes in me
Releasing my essence to flow upon the earth
Heavy the viscera deposited there
Stagnated eyes view creation
Out of plumb the world spins untrue
In phosphate skies crimson clouds run

In hope of no hope I tread the wire
Staring into the pit of my woeful shame
Dull existence threatens me
Death I do not desire
But peace is sought
In righteous quest I ride
Quiet ineptitude bars my way
Dim foresight crystal hindsight
Perplexes my condition
To stand and fall in anguished throws
Never to proclaim my love

Lost

John boats and jetties
Hot nights and teddies
Whisky and beer
Nights without fear
Warm rain on tin
Days without sin
Hot feminine sweat
Clothes once rent
Tides advance and recede
Sometimes taking what you need
Joyous tears when music flies
The world lies quiet tells no lies
Hope and faith trust to tell
The good heart that once fell
For want of love for want of gold
Naked finger naked soul
In blue moonlight love was sought
Lost now battle's cost.

Frozen

Snow freshly fallen
Downey white pillows cover earth

Fog frozen in thistle forms on branch and vine
Reflections of life echoed in grace
Silent but for the colloquy of trees
Dim illumination fortifies the dream space
But time and sun in death will bring
Wondrous vision to my eyes
Back to earth gelid forms retreat
Placating the fragile physicality
Of those who dwell upon her.

Retreat

Death's embrace granting eyes a welcome respite from grief
A rest until reborn to a world of distant virtue
My lonely heart quake's regarding conscience shaken
Remake the day with better things
Forward vision alight with latent imagination
To realize potential granted thus embodied mettle
Reclaiming life's hope to reign as true
Free will released to thrive unencumbered
An existence quantified through logic
Granted through artistic expression
To dwell with the gods of sanity and truth
Working without contention
Becoming whole anew

Killer

Pounding ineptitude inside your head
Where frightful yearnings gallop unchecked
Infertile thoughts seed your bed
Best left fallow the unchaste land

Craven wretch behind closed door
Quivering anticipation unabated now
Seeking a chance to step from his floor
To walk through threshold and dig with black plow

To rip and rend and tear apart
The firmament of dark mind's fever
Boiling blood pumps from dark heart
Sweet blood drips from raised clever

A killer is born of cold evils untold
A killer is free to roam the dark road.

Jig-Saw Man

The Jig-Saw Man is back in town
He'll cut your smile to make a frown
And leave you there in the dust
His hands stained with bloody rust

Native bride in bloody gown
Laying on the bloody ground
Trembling death in repose
The scent of it in his nose

The Jig-Saw Man is moving again
Watch out or he'll get you my friend
With vacant heart and dirty sleeve
A channel through you he will cleave

With absence of remorse abundance of nerve
Through evil of hatred to whom he serves
His kind will live to roam in the shadows
To slaughter those he considers cattle

Pothole

Oh pothole of massive girth
How small you were upon your birth
You grow larger every day
With each swallowed tire that comes your way

The springs and shocks of my truck
Are weaker now I curse my luck
With misalignment and dented rim
I go farther out on financial limb

I crave your death by filling in
Your cavernous mouth with blacktop skin
No one will miss you this I trust
Your fate is written in the dust

Although you will die one fine day
You will be back again this way
To devour our wheels in numbers untold
You terrible creature of unsmooth road

I Remember

I Remember...
Blue skies rainbows eyes and dragons on the wing
Dancing grass lightning flash walnut trees that sing
Muddy feet basketball beat a tree in Brooklyn grows
Willow trees skinned up knees a time I had no foes
Girls in skirts some that flirt and melodies that sing
My friend dog big bull frogs and flowers in the spring
Comic books things in nooks baseball cards in spokes
When Mountain Dew said" Yahoo" and times I laughed at jokes
I Remember...
The first July tomato eaten in the field
The tree house that I wanted that never did I build
Ponds and channel cats on straining line
Getting up at six to get to school on time
Ice cream bars Bart Starr the Beatles on TV
Mud between my toes one time bloody nose times when I felt free
Calves on bottles a rooster I wished to throttle a pair of soggy shoes
Thermometer under tongue bees that stung tooth I did not loose
I remember...
Superman Spider-Man the Hulk and Tarzan too
Mighty Mouse Underdog, Yogi and Boo Boo
Charlie Brown Cactus the clown the Fantastic Four

Batman E-Man Star Trek the Mighty Thor
8th Man Stingray Fireball XL-5
Captain America Sergeant Rock and Nick Fury will survive
Captain Kangaroo Mr. Magoo even Barney Fife
All of them together helped shape my life

Summer's Day

Singular but not alone
In a field I lie prone
My eyes turned skyward I watch the clouds
The show they give does me proud

The grass before me is a sea
My dog swims through it she sees me
We walk together to the woods
Small wildflowers and evergreen hoods

We explore hunt fight villains too
We see animals not housed in zoos
Some are friendly some are not
 None can hurt us that tree has rot

Strange sounds smells sights excite us
We grow tired but don't fuss
We sit a while gain our breath
We're tired not close to death

The sun hides behind that hill
We start back we crave a meal
As we walk home we pass the crops
We quicken our pace we smell pork chops.

Hannah Lewis

Only this life

The life the wife
Money Strife
Oh what we want

To have to hold
To give to take
Oh what we give

We live we learn
We must all take a turn
To bargain with the devil to give him his way

To earn to spend
To bend to lend
Oh what we will see

The life that is right the one that we choose
To live to give to cry to laugh
Happy sad wealthy poor

Mistakes

Still is the night cold is the chill
Cold is the ground wet are his boots
Long he walked down the lane alone
Only his thoughts will he have as companion

Sorry he is for what he has done
The yelling screaming snatching biting
What was he thinking or was he

Sweet Sixteen

Swinging from tress careless and free

Riding the bus shooting the breeze
Waiting for the moment the day you get your keys
Off to the movies a full tank of gas

Down the expressway careless and free
No thought of the danger that follows me
Crash the car hit a rail
The fun has ended the feeling passed

Riding down the road careless and free
Waiting praying for the day the roads I will see
A day when my life will once more be careless and free

A Diamond in the Rough

A diamond sheath
Masks the life
That longs for
A kiss of light
For natures arms
For the sky for warmth
My heart beseeches the Maker
For a stranger's smile
To end my
Resonant loneliness
With blissful light

Haunting

Straight the path
That leads me to the woods.
Dark the night bare the trees
The moon disappears behind the clouds
Wolves howl
Signaling the presence of an intruder
Snarling they move closer
Fearful I begin my trip back down the long path

The path has grown longer I am lost
Haunting are the sounds and shadows that follow
Lonely and scared am I
Dawn breaks I survive
I wonder as I wake what the new day holds
For it was only my dreams that frightened me

My love

My love my life
The one to have the one to hold
To give to receive
My partner in crime
Through the patch of love
A friend a foe
A lover a fighter
Through the harsh storms of life

Life

Life is long
Yet we are strong

Guide us now
For we are lost

Find a path
A fork in the road

Determine a direction
A path for life

Our souls have gone
For them we search

Death is near
We all have fear

Light

The window I gaze through is new to my eyes
For I have peered through these windows only since Sunday.
My bedroom window, portal to the outside
Behind the window I hide

The light seeps in, yet I am safe.
Safe from the hatred the world bears.
The sun's warmth reminds me, I am safe.

I remember

The long summer nights never ended
The short fall days with the tall bare trees
Only for myself will I have to fend
The days past I will remember always, the day ahead I cannot see.

I remember when I played till I could play no more
Played till my tiny limbs were sore
Oh for those days I long to play, oh the fun
Life is short I should have fun until my time here is done

The End of the Hare

The night is dark the trees are bare
Only the rumble of a small hare
He gallops the night by the light of the moon

Minutes pass, his life grows long.
His time has come, the birds sing a song,
A song of a short life come to and end
A sign from above, the world on the mend

Red, White and Blue

Red, white and blue are the colors we are fighting for
White the stripes between the blue
Blue the bed of stars

Red the blood to be shed
White the snow our soldiers long for on a hot desert day
Blue the day they went away

Red the face of the wind burnt soldier
White the eyes of the soldiers who stand and wait
Blue the feelings we all share

Donna Lee Campbell

Squaw Chief

She was old.
She was scary.
She was alone and wild.
They called her Squaw Chief

No one knew "her story,"
But, everyone knew "a story."
Her friends were the animals.
They called her Squaw Chief.

She had been born into a tribe
that was happy and robust
Her family was nothing special
Her father a warrior
her mother a squaw.

She was the oldest child.
She was adventurous.
Her father taught her everything,
the ways of the warrior.

He taught her to ride.
She was a natural.
He was surprised
and impressed.

He got her a pony.
She loved it.
She called him Sky.
They called her Squaw Chief.

Her father taught her to hunt.
Everyone was amazed
at her talent and natural skill
with bow and arrows.

One day watching his daughter,
The father found himself
Wishing his son had these skills.

He felt they were wasted on his daughter.

Even though she learned
The warrior ways from her father,
She still had to learn the things
A woman needed to know.

One day her Mother noticed
Children came to her daughter.
She answered their questions
And showed them how to do things.
They called her Squaw Chief.

Now she was older and
there was special boy,
one who came to visit
from another tribe.

He challenged her, but
Neither won.
Any game they played
They always tied.
They called her Squaw Chief.

When he had come and gone,
when his visit was over,
she was quiet and sad.
They called her Squaw Chief.

One day the shaman
called the men together.
He told them he had seen a vision.
He said a fog came and covered the
tribe.
When it lifted only skeletons were left.

He told the men to ponder this vision.
He told them that it was powerful
And that they need to know
What it meant.

There was a girl hiding and

Listening to the men.
They called her Squaw Chief.

That night, after everyone was
asleep,
the girl came to her father.
She told him she had heard what the shaman had said.
He turned and looked at her
In a way she had never seen.
He was angry!
She shouldn't have listened to the shaman.
He told her
"Never speak of it again!!!"

She went back to her blanket.
She quietly cried.
As they lay there,
The father realized
He had never heard her cry before.

The next day she was different.
She did not speak again.
She went off by herself.
She sat and listened to the sounds of the forest.
They called her Squaw Chief.

They asked her parents,
What was wrong?
The father knew but kept silent.
He didn't know
That he had hurt her spirit.

She began to dress different.
She made her own clothes.
She became separate from the tribe.
They called her Squaw Chief.

When the boy she liked came again to visit,
She seemed to return to her old self.
Then, she saw the strange people with him.
The white people.

The whole tribe gathered around the visitors.
They were curious of the white people
That's when it happened.

She began to walk through the crowd.
In her hand was a spear she had made.
No one had seen the spear before.
They called her Squaw Chief.

As she walked through the crowd,
They turned and looked at her.
They seemed to be under a spell.
They called her Squaw Chief.

She walked forcefully,
As if she was being drawn
To where she was going.
She walked past her love yet
Didn't see him.
That's when it happened.

She had her spear in her hand.
She raised it and
Plunged it into the chest
Of one of the white men.

No one did anything,
then all hell broke loose.
She had already turned and
made it to her pony, Sky,
hidden near the crowd.

The visiting tribe was yelling and
Fighting with her tribe.
The white people were screaming and
Wailing.
No one understood.

Then, just as she had come and gone,
The shaman appeared.
A calm came over everyone.

They looked to the shaman.

The shaman raised his hands high.
He said, "I know what the vision meant.
The white people are the fog.
The girl has saved our tribe
From being overcome and killed
By the white people.
The white people must go!"

The white people and the visiting
tribe
left. No one saw the girl again.
It became tradition to leave food and
blankets for her in the forest.

Sometimes at night,
While children sleep,
Feathers, rocks, and such,
Are left by their side.
They called her Squaw Chief.

Billy and Bobby

Billy and Bobby were twins
who lived down the street
I always thought they were cute
the kind of guys to meet

I was in the seventh grade
they were seniors in high school
I liked the way they looked
In my eyes they were so cool

School was out for summer
I walked around the block
I didn't see Billy and Bobby
I figured they worked around the clock

Then came fall
there was a bad storm
My family drove by their house
they were in military uniforms

My next door neighbor Dickie
was already in Vietnam
Did this mean they were going too
sad I started to cry

We ate dinner
watched the war on TV
It made me sick to think
that was where they could be

One day I came home
to find Mom looking out the door
worry in her eyes
she stood trying to see more

I went and put my stuff down
Came back and asked what was
wrong
Tears welled up in her eyes
she said we have to be strong

A man walking round the block
Billy and Bobby's Dad
Their unit had been hit
he was sad sad sad

They had served together
like the Sullivan brothers World War
II
Their family so upset
none of us knew what to do

Then word came from the Army
one dead and one alive
They didn't know which
All we could do was pray

I couldn't imagine this happening
that night the world was cold
I went to bed but couldn't sleep
Thinking of them I felt old

Finally news made it to us
Bobby was gone Billy was bad
I didn't know which was who
I just knew we'd lost what we had

I got older and married a Vietnam
Vet
Billy got better had a good life
We see him and talk of old times
He got a corvette but never a wife

Conversation with God

God what is the point
what is the reason for my existence
How do you feel about me
I have put up so much resistance

When you created me
What did you have in mind
Did you know this is what I would be
or did you think I'd be a different

Thank you for my blessings
I have many
Help me now to see
the steps to take if any

Yes Donna I know you
what you are within
You are my creation too
God counts the tears of all women

Easter with Mom

Easter with my Mother
Was always a pretty day
Even if it was raining
My Mother got her way.

Spring is a great season
New birth is everywhere
I love seeing baby birds
And flowers blooming.

Easter with my Mother
Meant an Easter basket
Easter eggs and lot of chocolate
Enough to put you in a casket.

The Easter outfit
Was very important too
Of course, white gloves
And a dress that's pale blue.

Easter with my Mother
Makes me smile still today
It was a holiday like no other
I want more Easters like yesterday.

Grandma Great

My Grandmother was perfect
she cooked and baked all day
One of seven children
her birthday is the first of May.

She made beautiful clothes and
played games with me so much
She loved and cared for me
I miss her sweet touch

When my son Eric was born
she became a Great Grandmother
That was a title she loved
She was like no other

After her death we missed her so
Yes even when we ate
My son sensed our loss
and said he too loved Grandma
Great

Hunting with Dad

Daddy's gone a hunting
Donna's going with him
She loves being in the woods
And being with her Dad

Daddy's gone a hunting
He's a good shot
Donna's got a gun
She knows a lot

Daddy's gone a hunting
He shot a rabbit
Donna's got to clean it
She's about had it

Daddy's gone a hunting
what is that sound
It's a rabbit crying
Donna's nowhere to be found

Daddy's gone a hunting
Daddy's gone alone
Donna's in the kitchen cooking
Donna stayed home

Sarizel LeFevers Robbins

Anger Garden

there is a dark place in my soul
an ugly dormant gaping hole

it lies in wait to take control
if sown with seeds of anger

with each new seed I drop within
a scraggly patch of weeds begins

with deadly thorns that pierce the skin
and spread the poison anger

straight from the devil's watering pot
it's forked tongue laps up the rot

that thrives on every unkind thought
and grows the seeds of anger

if I choose to let it go
its thorny weeds like kudzu grow

and bind me tight from head to toe
the parasite called anger

from every leaf a flower unfolds
in deepest reds and brightest golds

they're fueled by hell's hot glowing coals
these burning flowers of anger

they stab my heart and choke my soul
till the devil's vomit from me rolls

with hateful words out of control
since I fed the flowers of anger

I've seen it kill and hurt and maim
as it inflicts its chronic pain

I want no part of Satan's game
and I want no part of anger

God please send me angels bright
to kill hate's weeds with swords of light

in my garden I forever fight
this endless war with anger

teach me to keep my garden free
give me kind thoughts and place in me

a loving spirit toward humankind
a heart where one could never find

a garden spot for anger

Bomb Iraq?

bomb Iraq and SUVs
make us all
duct-taped plastic-wrapped
two-wheel drive four-cylinder
robots
after all...the earth is flat

Christmas Eve

I remember a fireplace on Christmas Eve
Grandaddy Ed in his easy chair
Nanny served custard and homemade cakes
we little ones ate from her best chinaware

electric blue candles cast magical light
on the scene of the Holy Nativity
reflecting the faces of those I loved
when Peace on Earth was reality

Note to Self

slow down   articulate
you know nobody gets it when you talk that way
slow down   celebrate
it's not an execution just another day

slow down   appreciate
embrace all things around you for they're gone so fast
slow down   anticipate
for each joyful here and now too soon becomes the past

looking back is often distorted
things tend to look perfect when they're over
remixed and digitally remastered
dead smiles frozen on each plastic cover

long as we're here the studio's still open
the instruments are waiting   plug them in
slow down   enjoy the music in each rough take
for we'll never play it quite the same again

Stopping Terrorism?

airport line...
longhaired guy
metal detector beep
think we'd better keep
this one long enough
to search his bags
looks okay to me
hmm what could this be
his metal-plated hand
souvenir of Vietnam
damn...
sorry for the inconvenience
meanwhile...
another man smiles
with briefcase and cane

he's boarding the plane
waiting for this chance
never got a second glance
a distinguished looking guy
the detector let him by
all the time he looked so nice
he was hiding a device
boom...
sorry for the inconvenience...

The Gypsy

the Gypsy danced into the fire
the coals were hot and white

her feet were bare she didn't care
she whirled to the crowd's delight

no sign of pain did she show them
not a grimace on her face

a dancer's poise and confidence
the epitome of grace

laughing she tossed her hair in the wind
she walked under the stars

unscathed by the world only
she knows the blisters the scars

The Saga of Mom and Me

Mom had an agenda
to be my agenda
The oldest of three
had to be me
Having only one girl

Mom mapped out my world
and tied it up
with a big pink bow

Mom told me to play
so on the first day
of first grade
I took lessons and played
I played the piano
I sang soprano
obtained finger power
practiced an hour
every single day
recorded by Mom
in a spiral notebook
she presented to
my piano teacher

"God gave you talent
and you are to use it
He'll take it away
if you ever abuse it"
said Mom to me
I had to agree
that it would be bad
if the talent I had
should get zapped away
when I'd practiced all day
it had to be true
since Mom said it

so I played for fun
for everyone
although I was small
I played for them all
the would be vocalists
the cultured localists
anytime anywhere
I had to be there
because Mom promised them
and God that I would

I have often wondered
where I'd be today
if I'd had no talent
or hated to play
would Mom have been sad
would she have felt bad
or would she have told me
that God gave my talent
to some other girl because
I didn't practice enough

I took last year off
since I'd played forty four
I wanted to see
if there was something more
something else I could do
that I'd chosen to
all by myself
without Mom

one day I woke up
and decided I should
teach piano
yes that would be good
couldn't wait to tell Mom
thought she'd be glad to hear
but she only replied
"you've not taught for a year
you probably can't play anymore
you know if you don't
use it you lose it"

This Moment

This moment is mine
to do with as I choose

before the web of time
makes me this moment lose

I'll keep this moment on a page
captured by my pen

May this moment some future day
rise and live again

Waiting

dark nights gray days
someone's songs already say
the things I would have said today
because I waited

from yesterday I tried to borrow
a little joy a little sorrow
to help me make it to tomorrow
and I'm still waiting

everything I do the more
it seems it's all been done before
is my life really such a bore
or is it me

tomorrow I'll get up and then
I'll try and start again
I'll find strength to say to do
the things I've always wanted to
yet then again   I may wait   wait   wait

Charlotte Irene Ingram

Child/Adult

As a child …I dated.
As a child…I married.
As a child…I came close to death.
As a child…I gave birth.
As a child…My soldier boy left.
As a child…Mother of three alone.
As a child…I grew.
As a child…War changes people.
As a child…I was an adult.

Lost/Revealed

When
someone I know…I love
walks out…vanishes
I'm affected, alone,
I've lost love.
I don't get over it.
I live with it…
I remember pain
I've a job to do, I gotta do it.

Images die,
I've lost a dream.
I have to get over it
My dream
Pain
No miracle here.

All is gone but not lost
you came…our time was short
you went you were quickly robbed
You didn't see the robber !

I saw it coming…Intimate
Life, thought, changes
Quickly done, swiftly programmed,

Overnight success.
No IQ...Barriers Gone
Lost sight, thought, life

life's not ours to keep

Yellow

Yellow births intelligence
Yellow helps one grow
Yellow is the sun bright
Yellow is the opening of night
Yellow true
Yellow not blue
Yellow opens my mind
Yellow is kind
Yellow is a rose
Yellow is a blessing to my nose
Yellow is an embrace
Yellow is a feather to my face
Yellow touches soft as cotton
Yellow can't be forgotten
Yellow opened doors that kept me from being rotten
Yellow is the color of my imaginary room
Yellow will make me what I want to be soon.

God's Given Nature Shows Hope

The temperature lowered, rain turned to sleet,
falling quickly, piercing the body.
Sunlight, ice glistened on the beautiful scenery.
Balls of ice, cut like a knife as life penetrates the heart.
Trees sculptured with drops of tempered rain,
leaning limbs weigh heavy with precipitation,
drops turn to flakes of
whirling snow.
With frigid weather , flowers did not bloom.

Grey skies vanished into golden noon. Loneliness ceased.
Ripening the wilderness of God's creation,
brown fell into pink, sleet was warmed by sun's delight.
The soul of a lonely man saddened by changing seasons,
gloomy, frigid, fierce , yet there's still hope.
With golden radiant beams, winter faded into spring.
God's given nature show's life a reason for Hope!

I REMEMBER...ALL ABOUT SCHOOL DAYS

I remember down the lane each morning I'd walk,
just me and the pebbles we'd have us a talk.
We'd talk of a mean teacher, with a bun in her hair,
and stuck up miss prisses, with their noses in the air.

I remember the bus ride to school every morn,
mean kids they would snicker, they'd laugh and they'd scorn.
Some bus drivers, they'd scream as if they'd bust a lung,
they'd act as if each student, should be strung up and hung.

I remember most adults forgot kids were humans and had feelings too,
as they'd snap their desk with rulers and threaten what they'd do.
They'd scream, papers and pencils on desk and write this ten times,
I will not do this or that and I'll stay in at recess when the bell
chimes.

I remember , oh yes, there were some happy school days,
when happy, laughing people were considered the gays.
It's funny how times and twisted imaginations change things,
like when little kindergartners were little angels with wings.

I remember the "The Ten Commandments" being taken off school
walls,
now doors need to be locked, golden rules left the halls.
Now schools have changed, prim and proper's not there,
go report to your seat , face many fears , and no one to cares.

I remember the hugs some teachers would give,

now it's hands off the students, so their job they can save.
Hot meals, meats , veggies, and homemade bread each day,
things of the past, now cold cuts and pizza are the way.

I remember when truth was truth and a lie was lie,
now students don't know the difference as they look you in the eye.
Yes, times have changed like good manners they went,
do you like what's become since "The Ten Commandments" were
sent.

I remember those pebbles were silent, they didn't gossip and tell,
they just laid there and listened, bout my bus ride from hell.
I'd kick up the pebbles, till garter snakes appeared,
with a look up the lane, my home was near.

* I have several friends who are teachers and they show as much love
and compassion in their classroom as the law will allow .

Back When

I remember back when ice cream cones and soda pops were five cents,
little cokes, big red machines, a slot where the nickel went.
Little candies were a penny, five cent candy bars,
somebody raised the prices, who do they think they are?

I remember playing kickball and great big swings at school,
riding in the back seat of the school bus was being cool.
Gasoline was a quarter a gallon, a loaf of bread was too,
A walk up town to the picture show, ten cents admission, fifteen for
popcorn, empty seats were few.

I remember when used cars were a hundred bucks,
Now used, that's looked down on, my that sucks.
Most transportation was your own two feet,
When you got tired, you'd rest by the creek.

Don't you wish you could go back when
a smile was a smile and nothing more then.
When people were kind and gossip was light

And you and your friends were tight.

I remember that little fist, laying money on the counter
to pay for the dolly that we found.
I remember first grade and waiting for the bus,
I thought she'd cry but she gave no fuss.

I remember middle school and her growing pains,
cheerleading tryouts, many goals she gained.
I remember high school, how nervous that first day she was.
Now her trampoline's empty, the house is too, time passes fast.

The first car came, the gasoline went fast,
Wanting help from parents to go out and have a blast.
I remember when we had to earn our own
monies, things were tight, there was no loan.

Christmas came, he bought her a ring.
She thinks she needs to get married cause that's the thing.
Marriage will come in time I say,
stop, think, listen, prepare for that day.

We went from Back When to Now Then.
50s, 60s, 70s, 80s, 90s, 00s.
I remember Back When.

Bridge Of Hope

Winter storms have taken a toll
Cold and desolate is the city
Work with thy hand giving blankets
Smile...Bring a Bridge of Hope
After several streets are passed
Aside a cot was set for a child
Giving a fire heat was spilled over
Warmth Brought a Bridge of Hope
Swing open a door from brutal cold
Physical needs are met
Outreach was consumed humanly

Feelings Gave a Bridge of Hope
Gathering of hands clasping tight
Hugs for the wayward friend
A pat on the back for your fellow man
Love Brought a Bridge of Hope.
If one of every two hands made
A difference in someone less fortunate
There would be a building of a
Bridge for the Hope of America

DEAR LORD

Dear Lord, Lift me out of ruts of routine that bog down spiritual
growth, give strength for new battles and temptations.
Dear Lord, Open and keep open my heart's door to you,
return to me your power that once by grace I knew.
Dear Lord, Forgive the sin that grieves your heart and keep me true.
Give me strength and wisdom to follow through.
Dear Lord, Make my path straightforward for you,
save my lost loved ones, touch sick friends, in Jesus' name , Amen.
Dear God, Thank you for sending Your only Son, to die on the cross
for this ungrateful one.
Dear God, Thank you from the bottom of my heart.
Please, Lord let me have a small part.
Dear Lord, Thank you sweet Jesus from my head to my feet,
one day in heaven face to face we'll meet.
Dear Lord, Thank you for the sun, moon, and stars,
for your loving arms around me and taking away scars.
Dear God, Thank you for heaven, where one day I'll be,
for my salvation, so warm, and so free.
Dear Lord, Thank you for the love notes written in red,
You're Alive, You're Alive, You're Not Dead.
Dear God, Thank you for reminding me, there's royalty in my family,
My Father is a King and He's also a Friend who loves me.

Satisfied Chief and Hunter

Chief, Husband, Father, Hunter

Red, orange, brown and black were the head feathers hanging to the
center of my back,
I earned each one from learning to fish, hunt and track.
I was taught as a boy how to live off the land and my ancestors' ways,
As a lad running free, those were great days.

The bright yellow sun shown cross the brown Prairies flat,
Heat so red hot it burned the ground where we sat.
We'd gather a circle or form a ring,
Chanted voices I heard from the Pow Wow while they sang.
We'd rise before sun-up to leave for the kill,
To provide food for our families and the Winter to fill.
A Brave in my headdress, I'd ride my spotted Palmetto so proud,
I knew I was a great hunter in this Cherokee crowd.

We'd slaughter, skin, clean and prepare.
Our hunt was successful for all it was fair.
The long journey back at daybreak we'd ride.
My hunt, I couldn't wait, to my lady I'd confide.

The sight of the teepees came into view,
As we arrived at our camp all were sleeping cept a few.
I ran to my door, untied the flap, I saw my wife and my son.
I had provided for them, I knew this hunt was good.

I watched as they slept, the moonlight glowed,
Their faces shown, much peace they did know.
I gathered my thoughts, laid my head to the ground,
A family, provision, love, and peace I have found.

OH, MAMA

I remember, Oh Mama, when I was three, my name I didn't know,
I wasn't sure if it was Att Att or if it was, No No.
I heard the words don't do this and don't do that,
Oh Mama, I didn't know rather to stand or sit or stay where I was.

I remember words like, you better answer me, just sit there and don't say a word,
Oh Mama, what is it you want me to do, I thought it was shut up that I heard.
I remember the screams, the smacks in the face, the yanking of my hair,
You said these things were done out of love, but I really don't think you cared.

Oh Mama I remember thinking if this is love please don't show me hate,
Yes, and Mama I remember you staying out nights till very late.
I remember crying and begging, Oh Mama please stay home,
I was scared at age eleven, for the two girls and me to be left alone.

I remember the two older siblings, to athletic activities they went,
As I pulled the chair up to the sink, to do dishes I was sent.
Oh Mama, I remember the divorce and how us five kids cried,
Please tell us Daddy, an explanation, please tell us why.

I remember the house became different, Mama she went to work,
Oh Mama if you and Daddy only knew how us five kids hid all our hurt.
I remember from brown bottles my Daddy drank,
Then with diabetes he got sick and went into a coma I think.

I remember Mama mixing sugar and water to form a paste,
On Daddy's chest she sat and shoved it in his face.
Oh those noisy sirens, the sounds that took our Dad away,
The tears us five kids and Mama cried on that sad sad day.

I remember the organ playing "Beyond the Sunset" that heart wrenching tune,
Oh Mama, this wouldn't be happening if love had been first for those six in the room.
Yes, I remember the sadness that made Mama pass out one noon,
My brother hit a parked semi and left two little girls too soon.

I remember a call from the Doctor at five in the morn,
He said you know your Mom's sickness, her attack was massive and torn.
Once again I remember the music, sad songs, tears and parting,

Our family got small early, leaving four adult girls with a new start.

Oh Mama, when us four girls get together, we seldom speak of childhood,
Cause we each remember things different, each memory is misunderstood.
You have three daughters now married, one divorced and saddened from choice,
If love was put first in families, there'd be reunions of happiness to rejoice.

DADDY

I remember the ole country house out that dark Benson Pike,
the grassy path where I rode my little red trike.
I remember blonde stringy hair and at the age of three,
running down the path my Daddy to see.

I remember the grasses where I got the bee sting,
Daddy's big arms tried comfort to bring.
I remember his hat, gray and tilted to one side,
his five children his wife he glowed with much pride.

I remember the crops, the doghouse out back,
How Daddy's hard work paid off, nothing we lacked.
I remember Ole Queenie, on her housetop I sat,
with red tomatoes or watermelons and see how far I could spit.

I remember Grand-Daddy got sick and we had to move,
the farm it was gone, now city life was the grove.
I remember lunches when Daddy came in to eat,
he was covered in grease from his head to his feet.

I remember one sad night a phone call came in,
my Daddy went to heaven I heard from my kin.
I remember as I grew up, Daddy wasn't around,
oh, how I missed those comforting arms in that big city town.

I remember getting upset with my friends talking bad

about their Daddy's and the home life they had.
I remember thinking, if they only knew how life is
without Daddy to talk to, advice, hugs from arms...only his!

With Love From: A Daddy's Little Girl*

*So if you have your Daddy, no matter your age, talk to him and think
of what's on this page.

I LOVED YOU ENOUGH

Written For: Timotha Chanaye Yeager
...I Loved You Enough
When I stayed awake through those long nights of teething
I sang "Silver Bells" and rocked you to sleep,
I walked around, held you close...I did everything
Even kept my patience when it was hard to keep.
...I Loved You Enough
To stand by to watch you stumble & fall
So you would gain courage to learn how to walk,
I tried to create excitement with every story I told
And I tried not finish your sentences when you began to talk.
...I Loved You Enough
To tell you~Don't touch those electrical plugs!
Don't play with matches! And Don't talk to strangers!
I told you to stay away from alcohol & drugs
Because I wanted to protect you from any possible danger.
...I Loved You Enough
To cook special foods the way you liked,
And taught you to look both ways while on your bike.
I found a church and took you to each service,
I wanted you to love the Lord, put Him first and not miss!
...I Loved You Enough
To read that same bedtime story
Until your eyes closed shut,
I didn't beat you when I screamed, "GOD! Why Me!"
As I scraped dried Play Dough from the carpet.
...I Loved You Enough

84

To tell you that practice makes perfect
No matter how good you think you are,
I took you to gymnastics and watched your back hand-springs per-fect
And encouraged and watched you cheer and traveled to games very
far.
...I Loved You Enough
To try to make everything right that's wrong
And fought back all my tears,
I gave you inspiration when I knew you weren't strong
To handle your griefs, sorrows, & fears.
...I Loved You Enough
To put footprints on the roof
And bake 12 dozen cookies...just because...
I couldn't handle telling you the truth
That there's no such thing as Santa Claus!
...I Loved You Enough
To give up my one-day-of-the-year to treasure
When I smiled and said, "Yeah! Sure, it's Okay!
Go with your father or mother to Great Adventure!
Even though it's Mother's Day!"
...I Loved You Enough
When you treated me bad
And ran me down to your friends and made me sad,
When you screamed at me from the top of your voice
"I'm eighteen now" and I knew it was your choice!
...I Love You Enough
To die the most painful death there is
And cry an ocean full of my tears,
Just as long as I never feel as upset like this
And come to some kind of terms in the upcoming years!
...I Love You Enough
I LoveYou more than words can express
Even when it's made my heart bleed,
So many times I told you, "YES!"
And sacrificed my own need!
I'd suffer~forever~in hopes you'd never know
Just how much your words have hurt me,
Because I Loved You Enough to say, "NO!"
And you were wrong for saying,
"YOU DON'T LOVE ME!"

With All My Love,Mom

Remember:

It's "Mommie", And... I Love You Enough...
To Stick Around And Be Here At Home,
And I'll Always Be Here For You Just Where You Left Me
If You Decide Here To Roam!

Hannah Rhea Marsh

Mato

(Man Killing Bear)

Black mask mastiff
Mato

Big, clumsy, protective
Safe

Fun, silly, fantastic
Laugh

Slobbers, snores, farts
Life

Company, heart, memories
Home

It's Time to Go Back to School!

It's time to go back to school
Even though the teachers treat us like fools
I'll try to do my best
Work real hard to pass each test
Its time to go back to school
Boo hoo!

My Big Sister, Emily

Not by blood but by love
Emily is great I thank God above
Pretty and smart like me
She'll be an attorney with her degree
I'll be a vet on this I bet
Different careers but sisters yet
We'll have nice apartments and fancy cars

We are both pretty and it's not from jars
Maybe when I grow up we will hang out more together
Can't wait till I am eighteen the sooner the better
As a sister she's great, when she picks out my clothes
I like what she chooses about style Emily knows
I love you Emily my sister and friend
Always buddies until the world ends

Our new baby

Another new baby
Sweet as can be
But not as lovely
As little ole me!

She has no feathers
But lots of quills
When going "potty"
She spills and spills

She wants to be held
All of the time
And if you don't
She thinks it's a crime

God places in our care
All sorts of babies
Shelter food shots
We do not want rabies

I love each of them
And their amazing feats
Thank you Jesus
Life is sweet

Sammy

Crying silent tears that no one but you can hear
Angels above invisible to me
But for you their presence is clear

Death is approaching you can feel it in the breeze
You climb into your bed silently
Clueless that your death brings me to my knees

Sammy I will always love you miss your sweet face
Forever asleep from which only God can awaken
Go with the angels to a sweeter place

Shad Smith

America the Beautiful

"Keep America Beautiful" Was the commercial of the day
And then the lonely Native American slowly rode away

I remember the tears streaming from his eyes
And I remember thinking a man not ashamed to cry

I was told he was an actor and his message but a game
 "He didn't love America, he only wanted fame"

I looked into his tears as a person would a stream
Lost in my reflection I soon began to dream

I saw myself standing in a mountain scene
I heard beside me movement but couldn't see a thing

Pollution had turned our blue skies grey
Mountains of garbage stood in my vision's way

Straining to see I saw her, a Bald Eagle on the ground
Her beauty left me speechless, and I couldn't make a sound

She was lost and out of place among the debris
But then I heard her thoughts, as though she spoke to me

Looking at her frozen for I did not dare to blink
It really is a miracle to hear an eagle think!

She only wanted water and a fish or two
But the trash that filled the river made it impossible for her to do

I thought "Now aren't I special?" to hear and fill her need
I gave to her some water and three fish on which to feed!

While eating she looked at me sadly and slowly told her story
In my mind I saw her soaring in all her glory

Her mate was shot for sport closing my eyes I saw him fall
Screaming she hunted for her nest but the tree was not there at all

Her nest was gone her eaglet too
Where to go? What to do?

Then my eagle started to tremble as if in sudden pain
I saw the truth in her eyes contaminated fish were not fair game

With eyes full of wisdom she said "I die without regret"
So you can tell my story and man will not forget

Now don't forget she told me as she spread her wings to fly
If man does not stop polluting soon all living things will die!

She never left the ground that day I stayed by her side
When she finally left me, I hung my head and cried

"Keep America Beautiful" I still hear the Native say
"So the mighty Eagle will never go away"

The Painting

My baby, is dying
Death in her eyes
The hard part is
For mommy to cry
I beg I plead baby don't go
For causing her more pain I'll hurt forever I know
She clings to my hand, squeezing it tight
And as it slowly loosens
I'm alone in our fight
 Two weeks ago, her elder sister died
 All my people cried and cried
Now my youngest daughter has gone away too
She said "Mommy my sister is calling
Wanting to play"
So now my babies are together
And I cannot understand
Enemies without hearts
A tribe called Wachucka! White man!
They had a general an **artist** so smart

With gifts of diseased blankets
He turned war into **art**
Fine art of killing done with a simple stroke
Uncle Sam this **artist** still laughs at his joke
He **painted** us as savages
 Part of his design
So many deaths
For land
The Trail of Tears his **framework**
Young and old all dying
Father Sky I beg of you "Please let it rain
So I know you too are crying sharing this pain"
Mother Earth I implore you
Since now I'm alone
Take away this anger turn my heart to stone!

Of the Delaware Nation

My Eagle

I met an eagle
Who flew straight
And true
Across my heart
He left me blue!
He would not lie
He could not stay
Shit happens
But why this way?
He took me soaring
With a single kiss
No matter what happens
He'll forever be missed
A president elected
Running the show
Sending our loved ones
But afraid to go
I ask the mighty spirit
Why this must be

He said eagles fight
To keep America Free

Red Apple
Far from the tree
I have
F
A
L
L
E
N

Red on the outside
White within
L
O
S
T

Rotten and Bruised
Crying, crawling
W
O
R
M
S

Hold me I'm alone
Sad memories
S
H
A
D

War is a thief

Mother Earth
As a virgin
 The first victim of war
Raped
Abused
Left feeling old
The child you birthed
Your rapist named "Gold"

Mother Earth
Unwed maiden
Uncle Sam wanted more
Rapist
Grinned
Called you whore
For a son "Coal"
Once again declared war

Mother Earth
Fertile woman
Broken
Forlorn
Plowed defeated
Raw wounds left untreated
Rivers of blood "Oil"

Memories of Grandma

Grandma
Kind, strong
Love without question
Alice

Grandma
Accepted me
Walked for miles
Joyful

Grandma

Christmas Eve
Filled with love
Home

Grandma
Gone ahead
With angels sings
Free

My favorite color
White

White the color of snow
White the moon aglow
White the car my enemy drives slow

White the Russians I drink
White my socks that stink
White the stars that blink blink blink

White the people who stole our land
White I am instead of tan
White I am because I am

White the house where I reside
White the world I am forced to abide
White the anger I keep deep inside

White my hair which once was black
White the lightning the sky attack
White the lie I live a fact

White the stripe on my skunk
White the tears I shed in a funk
White the world I get drunk

Youth

Once we danced
Found romance
Carved initials in a tree
All he did for me

Once we loved
Smiled laughed
Found joy in touch
Being free
All he did for me

Then the end
Lost lover friend
Gone like the initials in our tree
All he did for me

Pow Wow

Drums beat loudly
Dance

Native Americans finery
Feathers

Spinning, twirling, reaching
God

Together one
Love

I remember

I remember dreams, the reservation, flowers, trees, a life so sweet
Then of waking one morning to noise, rats and Cleveland streets

I remember the chief my father stealing then burning money and
going to jail
At sixteen life became hell

I remember finding my dreams at the bottom of a tequila bottle
Then becoming sister to the worms I swallowed

I remember writing my thoughts, memories to share
Then asking for help but no one was there

Dance with me?

My mom once danced with death in the form of a stranger
Protecting her offspring from evil from danger
I danced spinning slipping in the blood on the floor
Leaping to answer the pounding on the door

The bright disco lights flashing blue then red
Police cars, ambulance, "Is he dead?"
 Flash of camera recording the scene
Like an old scary movie on a silent screen

Too young to understand what the dancing stranger wanted
But for many seasons my mother looked haunted
 I remember my swaying to music only we heard
Exchanging songs love without voicing a word.

Kendall Road

Once upon a time
In the not too distant past
We were the only house
How I wish it could last

Neighbors came
To escape the city
They put in

Street lights, how shitty

Now out my window
I cannot see stars
Just a man made sun
And headlights from cars!

The streetlight reminds me
Of a stage and spotlight
So I make it a point
To dance naked at night!

I've been asked to refrain
From my exhibitionist itch
But I didn't install the spotlight
So who's the stupid bitch?

I'm easy to get along with
As you can plainly see
Get rid of the spotlight
Then you will not see me!

Exhausted from dancing
I climb into bed
With visions of moon and stars
Spinning in my head!

I miss their twinkle
And the glow of the moon
Instead at midnight
My room is as noon.

I wonder if I should charge
For my grotesque display
There would be no time limit
Since nights are the same as day

Smith and Jones

Last night I dreamed of rats with names Smith and Jones
They seemed like nice creatures we gladly shared our home
At first they asked for little
Food from our own hand
And if it were no trouble a tiny piece of land

We tried to teach them our ways to take only as you need
To kill a few buffalo but leave the rest to breed
We told them of Mother Earth and of Father Sky
We told them to treasure life, like children they asked "Why?"

They seemed like helpless children who would have surely died
Unless the "People" taught them skills how to survive
We reached out to them with hearts in hand
But pulled back stumps no fingers hope or land

At first there were a few but soon two was four
Before we knew it we could count them all no more
First they killed the buffalo then ripped the heart from Mother Earth
This shining rock called gold taught us what life was worth

The Great White Father spoke from both sides of his face
 To us he said "We're all brothers" to them "Kill that race!"
So White Father I ask you "Where will it end?"
And "How do you give to other countries, when there's nothing left to
spend?"

You tax your own poor to pay for your growing lust
They have nothing left to give but still you say they must
The river's are now polluted the air we breathe is black
You've civilized the red man, there is no turning back

You kill your unborn children then go about your day
One more little problem soon out of the way
Those born steal cheat and lie
They follow in your footsteps so please don't ask me "why?"

Now my people are more white than red our way of life a dream
I never look into a mirror for fear I will scream

I used to believe life was good but that is such a lie
It's better to walk with the Great Spirit than slowly die

Once again I lie down to sleep praying I might
Dream only of the beauty of an eagle in flight
But this never happens for soon I dream of smoke
And of many rats laughing at some simple private joke
Ding Dong the Witch is Dead
I looked into the mirror and cannot believe my eyes
I'm no longer eighteen more like eighty-five
Is that a gray hair surely not
I can't be getting old I'm too mean to rot
Looking closer wrinkles I see
How can old age be happening to beautiful lovely me
But yes I am dying and as I crumble into dust
My friends will say it's sad Shad never learned to trust
I know what they'll be thinking for this I've heard them tell
Shad will instantly combust she's to mean to burn in hell
There will be much laughing as they turn my home into a bar
Drunken they will draw straws on who will get my car
And the thousands of men who wanted me in their beds
They will say "Good riddance that bitch is finally dead"
I asked my partner in crime to take my ashes to Wounded Knee
She said "that's no problem you can depend on me"
Then picking up the broom I used to ride
She sweeps up all my ashes and tosses them outside
And as the humans start to leave my animal babies appear
And shed for me the first true tears
Kola my Macaw will curse Rhea Raccoon will cry
The Iguana dog and hedgehogs will ask each other "Why"
Upon my monument these words they will inscribe
Saint Shad has gone away to join her long lost tribe
And on this stone an angel will be placed
Giving the middle finger to the government of the white man's race
Truthfully I love all people almost as much as my babies
And I would have married a white man if I wasn't afraid of rabies
So without further ado I bid you all goodbye
I'd rather leave you laughing you're too ugly when you cry

Mom

You worry too much about one thing or another
You worry about your children especially my brothers
You worry about Little Phil will he sleep through the night
You worry about Mark and his are they eating right
You worry about Shad in college will she pass
You worry about Regina is she going to class
You worry about Mike a soldier alone
Wishing he were out and heading back home
Mom you worry too much you don't need this fright
We are your children you raised us up right
But mom you worry too much

Ron Whitehead

Springfield, Kentucky
October 15, 2002

visited Springfield
flew to Louisville
drove Bardstown Road to
St. Catharine College
then on to The Starving Artist Café

Welcome to Springfield, Kentucky

wandered   Main street   side streets
        lost   for hours
          small suitcase weighed down with
    heavy words
          The Emancipation Proclamation
          The Gettysburg Address
   Abraham Lincoln's words his works his life
        biography of his boyhood
    he was spiritual intuitive psychic

"That on the 1st day of January, A.D. 1863, all persons held as
slaves... shall be then, thenceforward, and forever free..."

and I'm searching for Abraham Lincoln
on Bardstown Road   Beech Fork   Lincoln Homestead

"Four score and seven years ago, our fathers brought forth upon this
continent a new nation: conceived in liberty, and dedicated to the
proposition that all men are created equal."

Welcome to Springfield, Kentucky   Abraham Lincoln country

I walked Kentucky   into the wind
    dark and bloody ground
    jewel in the lotus
    omphalos
    heart of the world
    holy triangle
    sacred

Abbey of Gethsemani   St. Catharine's   St.
  Joseph's
Trappist monks   Dominican nuns
coal mined   bituminous gold   nearly gone
smokestacks   power plants   largest shovel
  in the world
profane
Native Americans   pioneers   farmers   coal
  miners
          strong women
poets   writers   musicians

        in Kentucky music is mountainous

and I'm searching for Abraham Lincoln
    the greatest President of them all
        he saved us from ourselves

and here I am in Springfield
    heart of Kentucky
    Lincoln country

        who will save us now

and I'm searching for Abraham Lincoln
    maybe Edgar Cayce can help
        modern day prophet
            one of the great psychics of all time
            and from Hopkinsville, Kentucky

    maybe Muhammad Ali   "The Greatest"
        from Louisville
        maybe Muhammad Ali can point the way
            with his International Peace Center

    "float like a butterfly
        sting like a bee"

        oh Muhammad oh Muhammad
            will you please help me cause

I'm searching for Abraham Lincoln

and the rivers and creeks of Kentucky
Ohio, Kentucky, Mississippi, Barren, Big Sandy, Rough,
Elkhorn, Green
spray us with tears
of Mexican immigrants
who for forty days and forty nights have
stood
in the fields outside America's door
knocking   denied entry   denied
Churchill Downs   The Derby
singing
"My Old Kentucky Home"   knocking
on our doors   pleading   "let us come in"
"let us live in your beautiful Kentucky Home"

and I'm searching for Abraham Lincoln

walking up hills   mountains   The Knobs   The Appalachians   Natural
Bridge
bowing to gravity
leaning backward with my long hair sweeping the path
as I descend the wind and the descent flatten me
and now my muscles are green and yellow and red pain
sustaining my search
drink wine and strong coffee
at The Starving Artist Café

and I'm searching for Abraham Lincoln

I want love to have its way
I want us to stand united   not divided
One world One people   together   in peace and harmony

and searching for Abraham Lincoln
I crawl through Kentucky
so many diamonds I find   birthed from the deep dark mines
Iroquois Cherokee Shawnee Tribes   Daniel Boone   Henry Clay
Abraham Lincoln
Elizabeth Madox Roberts   James Still   Bill Monroe
Loretta Lynn   Muhammad Ali   Hunter S. Thompson
Johnny Depp
Harry Dean Stanton   Ned Beatty   Adolf Rupp

111

                    Rick Pitino   Lionel Hampton   Wendell Berry
          John Jacob Niles   Pee Wee Reese   The Everly Brothers
        Merle Travis   Rosemary Clooney   Edgar Cayce
              Robert Penn Warren
          the literary renaissance   Thomas Merton   Judy Morris
        Appalshop   Bluegrass   Bourbon   Beautiful Women
                    My Old Kentucky Home   Churchill Downs
              Louisville Slugger
        The Great Outhouse Blowout   Penn's Store   Gravel Switch
                Kentucky Fried Chicken   Wildcats   Cardinals

                          and as I search for Abraham Lincoln
                          I sit in The Starving Artist Café
                          on a rainy October day
                          drinking wine

                          why do men still drink wine
                          and women still water

                          beautiful paintings cover the walls
                          and yes when I give readings round the world
                          I hear 3rd world voices monks and nuns
                                    Ernesto Cardenal   Nicanor Parra
                                    Daniel Berrigan   Thomas Merton
                                    Mother Teresa   Judy Morris
                                          The Dalai Lama
                          pierce the world's terrors chanting singing praying
                                                for love
                                                for peace

                          and I'm searching for Abraham Lincoln
                          "the one who'll shake the ones unshaken
                          the fearless one"

                          and searching for Abraham Lincoln
                                in the St. Catharine College Library
          I look in Lawrence Ferlinghetti's   yes San Francisco
          Ferlinghetti who stood
                    At Merton's grave with me
              I look in Ferlinghetti's A Coney Island of the Mind and

                    and I read

          "Christ climbed down
           from His bare tree
           this year
           and softly stole away into
           some anonymous Mary's womb again
     where in the darkest night
           of everybody's anonymous soul
           He awaits again
           an unimaginable
           and impossibly
           Immaculate Reconception
           the very craziest
           of Second Comings."

                    and I'm standing in The Starving Artist Café
                    on Main Street in Springfield, Kentucky
                              the heart of Kentucky
                              the heart of the world
                    on this rainy Tuesday October 15, 2002
                    and the wind and the rain whisper
     welcome   welcome   welcome
                    to Springfield

     and I'm searching   searching   searching for Abe   Honest Abe
                              searching for Abraham Lincoln
                    in Springield

          welcome to Springfield, Kentucky USA

presented Starving Artist Café
Springfield, Kentucky
October 15, 2002

CALLING THE TOADS
THE ANTINOMIAN FIRE THIS TIME

By John Tytell and Ron Whitehead

the bone man dances circles
round the subterranean gloom
paints pink and blue and purple
until he fills the room
with the smell of roses
and a pandemonium moon

There is a struggle going on for our minds the minds of The World People. Every form of expression is being attacked. The attack is overt and subtle, explicit and implicit. The attack manifests as silent persecution, as mind manipulation, as censorship, as fear. The attack is pervasive. Most people, being asleep, are not even aware of the attack - until their doors are broken down. In the face of fear the poet the writer the artist the composer the musician the filmmaker can and must speak must act. I believe in individuals who are awake who fight for freedom. I believe in non-violent fighting which creates new forms new voices which, by their own being and expression and action, stand against reaction against fundamentalism against violence against war.

UNSCREW THE LOCKS FROM THE DOORS
UNSCREW THE DOORS FROM THEIR JAMBS

Anne Hutchinson, William Blake, Walt Whitman & The Antinomian Tradition

VOICES WITHOUT RESTRAINT

"Government shall make no law respecting an establishment of religion, or prohibiting the free exercise thereof; or abridging the freedom of speech, or of the press; or the right of the people peaceably to assemble, and to petition the government for a redress of grievances."

Anne Hutchinson, cousin of John Dryden, organized a circle of women and led them in discussions of church sermons. The notion that women would even dare to discuss these sermons was considered subversive - after all, discussion leads to questions. Anne Hutchinson was convicted of "traducing" the ministry and banished, cast out of Boston.

Antinomian emerges from the Protestant Reformation which encourages its adherents to deny authority and resist the state when its moral position is feeble, contradictory, absurd. In legal terminology an antinomy signifies a contradiction which in Walt Whitman's historical moment was the condition of slavery in a supposedly free society.

"The attitude of great poets is to cheer up slaves and horrify despots" Whitman wrote. He, like William Blake before him, saw his purpose as spreading to the people the original ideas of the American republic, and a revolution that had been fought to relocate sovereignty in the individual rather than in the state. In an editorial he declared that the greatest evil was "strife for gain," yet even in his crusading journalism he was a voice of affirmation and love.

"Unscrew the locks from the doors.
Unscrew the doors from their jambs"
(Whitman).

"Poetry fettered fetters the human race"
(Blake).

"It is not metres, but a metre-making argument that makes a poem"
(Emerson).

"Urge and urge and urge. Always the procreant urge of the world"
(Whitman).

"through the windr of a wondr in a wildr is a weltr
as a wirble of a warbl is a world"
(Joyce).

When Whitman completed LEAVES OF GRASS, the grass being the uncut hair of the dead, he designed it, set some of his own type, and set as has publication date the fourth of July, 1855.

LEAVES OF GRASS was disdained by critics as "a mass of stupid filth," an example of "New York Rowdyism," "grotesque and uncouth."

The only favorable reviews were written by Whitman himself, pseudonymously, except that is for a letter from Emerson proclaiming Whitman's book as the "most extraordinary piece of wit and wisdom that America has yet contributed." After Whitman was debilitated by stroke the young Henry James attacked his work and a generation later, in a jealous attempt to dethrone the cosmic poet who had written the American epic poem of the 19th Century, Ezra Pound continued the attack on Whitman's romanticism.

Whitman revised and expanded his poems for the rest of his life but not before paying over six hundred visits to hospital wards during the American Civil War. Basic surgery was amputation. Suffering was overwhelming. Whitman maintained cheerful optimism, the hallmark of his character. Whitman gave succor to the wounded.

Pound's CANTOS reflect his own lifetime of antinomian resistance to the warfare state. Long after he made his peace with Whitman, Pound became pariah of modern poetry, hysterically protesting "a system which created one war after another in series in system." Ezra Pound was incarcerated, twelve years in the house of bedlam, St. Elizabeth's, an asylum for the criminally insane in Washington D. C., which, years earlier, during the Civil War, had been one of the hospitals for the wounded visited by Whitman.

Another antinomian, arriving in Paris, 1930, with ten dollars and a copy of LEAVES OF GRASS, forty years old, twenty unsuccessful years trying to write fiction during an anguished marriage, liberated himself from the middle class values most take for granted, destitute, surviving by persuading a dozen new friends to feed and house him in rotation in exchange for his conversation, fell in love with Anais Nin, another unknown writer, and began his first masterpiece, TROPIC OF CANCER.

In his poems Whitman simultaneously praised and condemned his country. In CANCER Henry Miller savages America as a "cesspool of the spirit," "a curse on the world." While Whitman introduced orgasmic potential in "Song of Myself" Miller used sexual liberation as antinomian metaphor. Published in Paris, 1934, CANCER didn't appear in an American edition until 1960 when Miller was past 70. Whitman's poems were challenged by the district attorney of Boston but Miller's CANCER faced 50 obscenity charges resolved finally by the Supreme Court. One of the triggers of the Sixties.

Ezra Pound, an iconoclast far on the right of the political spectrum. Henry Miller, a Nietzchean nihilist with an anarchistic distrust of all institutions.
Both romantics who cannot believe with Whitman in the dream of American possibility.

Whitman, Pound, Miller, all Voices Without Restraint. Crucial American influences on The Beat Generation. The Beat Generation. In the next decade The Beat Generation will come to be recognized as the most important group of poets and writers in the history of America. Jack Kerouac, spokesperson for The Beat Generation wrote a panoramic rhapsody infused with Whitman's identification with the common, the lowly, the downtrodden. Kerouac eulogizes his hoboes and wanderers in the same natural speech which caused James Russell Lowell to keep Whitman off the shelves at Harvard. Kerouac's prose line, his long, endlessly unpunctuated, surging, sentences are based on Whitman's "Song of Myself" and like Whitman Kerouac is a celebrant who remains optimistic, despite all odds, despite all suffering struggle pain failure, he remains optimistic because he knows the journey is perpetual and has no end.

Kerouac's friend Allen Ginsberg is even closer to Whitman. "Howl," written exactly a century after "Song of Myself," uses the same long line. In Whitman's case as in Ginsberg's form becomes a function of the freedom to which the poet aspires. The holy, holy, holy, everything is holy is magnificent Whitman AH and AHA ecstasy.

Ginsberg is less ambivalent than Whitman about the human price we pay for commerce and industry, more in accord with Pound and Miller in his suspicion of Moloch, his cannibal dynamo of industry named after the Babylonian god to whom children were sacrificed. But Ginsberg's antinomianism has been, like Whitman's the wound dresser, adhesive, sewing a communal purpose. So Ginsberg helped organize the peace marchers in the Sixties, was witness to the Chicago National Convention in 1968, along with his friend William S. Burroughs, who may be the most antinomian of all The Beats.

Lawrence Ferlinghetti, who was arrested for publishing "Howl," Ferlinghetti, whose City Lights Books is antinomian mecca of the world, Ferlinghetti, whose A CONEY ISLAND OF THE MIND has sold more copies than any book of poetry by any living American poet, Ferlinghetti, antinomian to the end, sees the poet as enemy of the state.

The antinomian legacy of Whitman, Pound, Miller, Kerouac, Ginsberg, Burroughs, Ferlinghetti, and so many other poets, writers, artists, musicians leads to our door and in this final moment having stood in the shadows for too long we step out and now we stand on the

brink on the edge
at the ending of time
Time was, Time is, Time will be no more
and it's The Big Bang Epiphany
in the gap between thought and image
Voices   streams racing
whispering through our blood
pleading through our bones
strange activities of our nerves
the unconscious life of our minds
a tetrameter of iambs marching
shouting   Voices   Without Restraint
Alchemically Transmutative Symbol Decipherment
The Book as Sacred Elixir
Manger du Livre   Eat The Book

The shortest distance between two points is a creative distance

and Allen Ginsberg howls
"I saw the best minds of my generation destroyed by madness,
starving, hysterical naked"

and Diane di Prima rants
"the only war that matters is the war against the imagination, all other
wars are subsumed in it"

and Amiri Baraka chants
"They have turned, and say that I am dying. That I have thrown my
life away. They have left me alone, where there is no one, nothing,
save who I am. Not a note nor a word."

And Lawrence Ferlinghetti paints PICTURES OF THE GONE
WORLD

Allen Ginsberg   Diane di Prima   Amiri Baraka   Lawrence
Ferlinghetti

118

Numinous howls and rants and chants and paintings

and years of tears come fiercely flowing streaming
all the pain   wells up
years of failure   of not being enough for anyone
years of wandering   lost   on the outside
    Outlaw
being told "you ain't shit   you don't fit   what the
Hell you doin here? all you've done is create pain and sorrow
wouldn't you be better off dead?"

turning away from   walking away from   disappearing from
    Authorities   the past
The Dead

in the hermetic corridors of authority The Dead
somberly splash in their shallow sewers
devouring and regurgitating themselves
and with tears in my eyes a snarl on my lips and peace in my heart
I'm failing as no others dare fail
and I'm in the gap between thought and image
how'd I get here after all the years of not being self
after all the years of being   Other
of floating out of my body   on the ceiling
watching skin blood bones nerves   going through the motions
believing in space and time without realizing I was already
    Out   out of sync   beyond chaos
    breathing rhythms   at the ending of time
    and now   here   in the gap between thought and image
    where the only distance is creative distance
Here   Now   at The Ending of Time
I focus all three eyes   in wolf fashion
Closing Time
I walk through the stone called lump of fat
and I float through the fire that is central
and I enter the upper chamber of the golden pyramid
the confluence of all streams
polyglot commingling of all voices
Thalass feeds herself
and as I float over the open sarcophagus
I am
The Ocean of Consciousness

Knut Hamsun, progenitor of modernism, recipient of the 1920 Nobel Prize for Literature, in his 1890 essay, "On The Unconscious Life of The Mind," said "We would experience a little of the secret movements which are made unnoticed in the remote places of the soul, the capricious disorder of perceptions, the delicate life of fantasy held under the magnifying glass, the wanderings of these thoughts and feelings out of the blue: motionless, trackless journeys with the brain and heart, strange activities of the nerves, the whispering of the blood, the pleading of the bone, the entire unconscious life of the mind."

Art is a kind of innate drive that seizes a human being and makes her or him its instrument. The artist is not simply a person acting freely, in pursuit of a merely private end, but one who allows art to realize its purposes through her or his person. Artists have moods, free will, personal aims, but as artists they are bearers of a collective humanity, carrying and shaping the common unconscious life of the species.

So what, so what is the ocean of consciousness?

"The only war that matters is the war against the imagination,
all other wars are subsumed in it."
Diane di Prima

The psychic makeup of creative persons attracts attention, but the actual artistic achievement is the bedrock of inquiry when it is directed toward understanding the artist, for the artistic disposition adheres to a charisma that attaches to the 'office' and has collective aspects.

"To be an artist is to fail, as no other dare fail."
Samuel Beckett

Today 'Specialization' is sold on every corner, fed in every home, brainwashed into every student, every young person. We are told that the only way to succeed, here at the beginning of the 21st Century is to put all our time, energy, learning, and focus into one area, one field, one specialty (math, science, computer technology, business). If we don't we will fail. We are subtly and forcefully, implicitly and explicitly, encouraged to deny the rest of who we are, our total self, selves, our holistic being. The postmodern brave new world resides inside the computer via The Web with only faint peripheral recognition to the person, the individual (and by extension the real global community), the real human being operating the machine. The idea of and belief in specialization as the only path, only possibility, has sped up the fragmentation, the alienation which began to grow rapidly within the individual, radically reshaping culture, a century ago with the birth of those Machiavellian revolutions in technology, industry, and war. And with the growing fracturing fragmentation and alienation comes the path - anger, fear, anxiety, angst, ennui, nihilism, depression, despair - that, for the person of action, leads to suicide. Unless, through our paradoxical leap of creative faith we engage ourselves in the belief, which can become a life mission, that regardless of the consequences, we can, through our engagement, our actions, our loving life work, make the world a better, safer, friendlier place in which to live. Sound naïve? What does this have to do with Voices Without Restraint? With The Beat Generation? With the so-called and sadly mislabeled Generation X? With The Youth of Today? What place does The Antinomian Voice, The Voice of The Beat Generation, The Voice that, though trembling, speaks out against The Powers That Be, what place does this Outsider Poet Voice have in the real violent world in which we are immersed? Are we too desensitized to the violence, to the fact that in the past Century alone we have murdered over 100 million people in one war after another, to even think it worthwhile to consider the possibility of a less violent world? Are we too small, too insignificant to make any kind of difference? The power-mongers have control. What difference can one little individual life possibly make possibly matter?

Today the X and microserf generations are swollen with young people yearning to express the creative energies buried in their hearts, seeping from every pore of their beings. They ache to change to heal the world. Is it still possible? Is it too late? Is there anyone (a group?) left to show the way to be an example? To be a guide? A mentor? James Joyce, King of Modernism, said the idea of the hero was nothing but a damn lie that the primary motivating forces are passion and compassion. As late as 1984 people were laughing at George Orwell. Today, as we finally move into an Orwellian culture of simulation life on the screen landscape, can we remember passion and compassion or has the postermodern ironic satiric deathinlifegame laugh killed both sperm and egg? Is there anywhere worth going from here? Is it any wonder that today's youth have adopted Jack Kerouac, Allen Ginsberg, William S. Burroughs, Herbert Huncke, Gregory Corso, Neal Cassady, Lawrence Ferlinghetti, Amiri Baraka, Robert Creeley, David Amram, Diane di Prima, Ed Sanders, Anne Waldman, Bob Dylan, and all the other Beat Generation and related poets, writers, artists, musicians, photographers, filmmakers as their inspirational, life-affirming antinomian ancestors?

121

These are people who have stood and still stand up against unreasoning power/right/might, looked that power in the eyes and said NO I don't agree with you and this is why. And they have spoken these words, not for money or for fame, but out of life's deepest convictions, out of the belief that we, each one of us, no matter our skin color our economic status our political religious sexual preference, all of us have the right to live to dream as we choose rather than as some supposed higher moral authority prescribes for us.

In the next decade The Beats will come to be recognized as the most important group of poets and writers in the history of America. The Beats have given birth to new generations to new energies which are waking to the realization that the creative imagination provides salvation from suicide, from death in life, by revealing that there are alternative paths to explore in this world alternative paths that lead away from the mundane, the superficial, away from submission to mediocrity alternative paths opening into the inspired brilliant fire called LIFE.

The hallowed doors of Academia, Academia, the bastion of conservative thought, the doors of Academia are finally creaking open (just as it took so long for them to open to James Joyce, Virginia Woolf, Samuel Beckett and all other original thinkers and expressionists) the doors are creaking open and, finally, at least a discourse on The Beats has begun.

"I am more than my physical body and as such
I can see more than the physical world."
Robert Monroe

produce produce produce
young people of all ages
let go your fears
embrace failure
take risks
accept responsibility for your actions
embrace failure
through failure you will know undreamed of success

Mysticus Memoria Rhythmus:
Ignis Fatuus?

weaving wisps of memory beyond the thread of time
ocean of the forgotten fleet
with mystic memory rhyme
unseen siren sing within the pilfered soul
orchestrated rhythms of wind and drum
ride the blood crest
to the heart
move with word-thoughts distant
touch the untouchable emotion womb
cordate-chord at the core
of OM

If history is the embodiment of "fear, reason, social convention, and tradition" then it becomes the duty, the responsibility, the compelling creative urge of the Nabi, the Prophet, to crack history's encrusted, iconostasic, shell releasing the dying and dead by invocation of The Word, pure thought, translated via pure energy into meaning full sound. The Prophet, whose home is in Shadow in The Holy Unholy The Sacred and The Profane Realms of The Creative Imagination, as the synaptic link between spirit and matter, creates a new, enlightened awake being awake world.

Out of the postmodern surreal chaos will evolve a structure, more vast than presently perceivable, that I call The Ocean of Consciousness. The structure is difficult to perceive because we are the structure. We are the synthesis. All streams of thought of con and unconsciousness flow to our Ocean of Consciousness, the structure that gives birth to, engulfs, encloses, creates, and expands the chaos. Where do We, do I, my Self (all of me including my Spirit and Soul), begin and end? Do we begin? Do we end? The earth was once thought of as the center of the universe but our view, our perception, thrown out, into The Creative Imagination, like a boomerang, expanded, and is now returning and we will soon see that We, each One of Us, are the center of a vast, interconnected, perhaps infinite, universe.

My quest to reach beyond Modernism and postmodernism to The Ocean of Consciousness may be partially defined as a literary scientific alchemical mysticism in which the mysterium tremendum is alive and doing well. It is a creative, numinous attempt to reach a Fourth Kingdom beyond but encompassing the alienated and alienating realms of spirit, matter, chaos, a Fourth Kingdom wherein lies the synthesis of apparently irreconcilable differences. The journey is inward, outward, centered, liminal, in the heart, and on the edge to silence, to the immaterial, psychological, emotional, mental, spiritual self, but also simultaneously to the spoken, visual, material, the world of action. But the emphasis of the journey is inward with self soul consciousness at heart.

Knowledge, from the inception of Modernism (and through postmodernism and Chaos to The Ocean of Consciousness), is reorganized, redefined through Literature, Art, Music, and Film. The genres are changing, the canons are exploding, as is culture. The mythopoetics, the privileged sense of sight, of modern, contemporary, avant-garde poets, musicians, artists, filmmakers are examples of art forms of a society, a culture, a civilization, a world, in which humanity lives, not securely in cities nor innocently in the country, but on the apocalyptic, simultaneous edge of a new realm of being and understanding. The mythopoet, female and male, returns to the role of prophet-seer by creating myths that resonate in the minds of readers, myths that speak with the authority of the ancient myths, myths that are gifts from the shadow.

presented by John Tytell & Ron Whitehead, with piano accompaniment by David Amram, at The New York Underground Music & Poetry Festival, November 2000, NYC.

About The Twelve Kentucky Poets

Cathy Gilbert is active in humane treatment of animals and protecting the environment.

Ken Hageman is thirty-five years old Iowa Native, youth consolers wane be. Expressively deep, yet simple. "Been there done that, just want to give something back."

Jessica Patterson's life is animals and literature; She works for a veterinarian, owns a small horse farm. Her every spare moment is spent reading and writing-writing-writing.

Alex (Bear) Lanter is an artist, inventor and author.

Hannah Lewis is a native of Campbellsburg, Kentucky and has written the poems in this book for pleasure and hope readers receive the same pleasure.

Donna Lee Campbell lives in LaGrange, Kentucky. She is married to Bell Campbell and is mother to Eric and Tara. She loves the arts.

Sarizel LeFevers Robbins is a pianist and piano instructor who lives in Carrollton, Kentucky with her husband Ken and cat, Jude.

Charlotte Irene Ireland was born to Jack and Dorothy Ireland from Shelby Co, Kentucky and married Donnie Ingram. They reside in Henry County where they raised their children Don Jr., Dana and Chaye.

Hannah Rhea Marsh is twelve years old and a student at Carroll County Middle School.

Shad Smith is a Native American of the Delaware tribe, a veteran and President of the Carroll County Wildlife Recovery Program.

Ron Whitehead is the Professor of life for thousands of fans he is called the Medicine Man. Ron resides in Louisville, Kentucky with his wife Nancye.